Oman Travel Guide 2023

Muscat City, Beaches, Mountains, Deserts and Adventure: The Ultimate Oman Experience and must-see sights

ROLAND RICHARD

Copyright 2023. Roland Richard.

All rights Reserved!

No part of this book may be reproduced, stored in a retrieval system, or transmitted in any form or by any means, electronic, mechanical, photocopying, recording, or otherwise, without the prior written permission of the copyright owner.

Table of Contents

TABLE OF CONTENTS — 3
INTRODUCTION TO OMAN — 5
    OVERVIEW OF OMAN — 5
    HISTORY AND CULTURE — 10
    CLIMATE AND WEATHER — 16
PLANNING YOUR TRIP — 21
    THE BEST TIME TO GO — 21
    VISA CONDITIONS — 22
    TIPS FOR HEALTH AND SAFETY — 23
    EXCHANGE RATES AND MONEY — 26
    OMAN'S TRANSPORTATION — 27
EXPLORING MUSCAT — 31
    HIGHLIGHTS OF MUSCAT CITY — 31
    SULTAN QABOOS GRAND MOSQUE — 35
    CORNICHE AND SOUQ OF MUTRAH — 37
    MUSCAT'S ROYAL OPERA HOUSE — 39
    BAIT AL ZUBAIR MUSEUM — 40
COASTAL DELIGHTS — 43
    SOHAR — 43
    SUR AND THE TURTLE RESERVE — 46
    WADI SHAB — 49
    PENINSULA OF MUSANDAM — 53
    SALALAH AND THE REGION OF DHOFAR — 57
MAJESTIC MOUNTAINS — 62
    JEBEL SHAMS — 62
    JEBEL AKHDAR — 67
    AL HAJAR MOUNTAINS — 70
    NIZWA AND BAHLA — 72
DESERT ADVENTURES — 77
    WAHIBA SANDS — 77

- THE EMPTY QUARTER, OR RUB' AL KHALI — 80
- BEDOUIN CUSTOMS AND CULTURE — 81
- CAMEL TREKKING AND DESERT CAMPING — 83

CULTURAL EXPERIENCES — 85
- CASTLES AND FORTS — 85
- CUSTOMARY OMANI FOOD — 87
- FRANKINCENSE TRAIL — 89
- OMANI TRINKETS AND CRAFTS — 91
- CUSTOMARY FESTIVALS IN OMAN — 92

OUTDOOR ACTIVITIES — 95
- SNORKELING AND SCUBA DIVING — 95
- DOLPHIN OBSERVATION — 97
- TREKKING AND HIKING — 98
- ROCK CLIMBING — 100
- WATERSPORTS — 102

PRACTICAL INFORMATION — 105
- LODGING — 105
- INTERNET AND COMMUNICATION — 107
- REGIONAL PROTOCOL AND CUSTOMS — 108
- KEY ARABIC EXPRESSIONS — 110
- USEFUL CONTACT — 111

APPENDIX — 113
- OMAN TRAVEL TIPS — 113
- PACKING LIST — 114
- RECOMMENDED READING — 116
- MAPS OF OMAN — 117
- CONVERSION CHARTS — 118

Introduction to Oman

Overview of Oman

Oman, a nation on the southeast coast of the Arabian Peninsula, is a place of spectacular natural beauty, historic forts, bustling souks, and friendly people. Oman has grown to be an intriguing vacation destination for anyone looking for authenticity, natural beauty, and cultural experiences while being less well-known than its neighbours.

The United Arab Emirates to the northwest, Saudi Arabia to the west, and Yemen to the southwest form Oman's borders. Its coastline, which spans along the Arabian Sea and the Gulf of Oman, provides chances for water sports as well as gorgeous beaches and vivid coral reefs. Rugged mountains, enormous sand dunes, and lush wadis (riverbeds) are features of the interior of the country that contrast sharply with the coastal areas.

Oman's dedication to protecting its natural environment and cultural heritage is one of its most notable features. Due to the government's endeavours in sustainable tourism, carefully planned development that balances the preservation of traditional architecture and cultural places with contemporary infrastructure has been produced. This strategy enables tourists to enjoy contemporary conveniences and luxuries while getting a true sense of Oman's identity.

The nation's commercial and cultural centre is located in the capital city of Muscat. Muscat's scenic corniche, magnificent mosques, and old-world districts serve as examples of how tradition and progress coexist peacefully. Oman provides a wide range of adventures outside of Muscat. Each area of Oman has its own distinct appeal, from the historic dhow-building village of Sur to the ancient city of Nizwa with its majestic fort and busy souk.

The population diversity of Oman enriches its rich cultural fabric. Visitors should anticipate being welcomed with sincere compassion and respect because the Omani people are renowned for their warm hospitality. Through the decades, ancient Omani habits and practises have been passed down, giving insight into the country's rich history. Examples include wearing dishdasha (traditional clothing), engaging in the frankincense trade, and mastering the technique of falaj irrigation.

In addition to its efforts to safeguard its natural resources, Oman is dedicated to sustainable tourism. There are many environmental reserves in the nation, including the breathtaking Wahiba Sands desert, the lush surroundings of Jebel

Akhdar, and the Daymaniyat Islands' rich marine biodiversity. These places provide chances for environmentally friendly excursions like hiking, camping, wildlife watching, and diving.

Oman has something to offer, whether you're looking for a relaxed beach vacation, an outdoor adventure, or both. Its unique combination of scenic beauty, historical significance, and friendly hospitality makes it a memorable tourist destination that continues to enthral visitors from all over the world.

History and Culture

Oman has a rich and diverse past that dates back thousands of years and has been influenced by several civilizations and influences. The nation served as a centre for trade and cultural interactions due to its advantageous location along historic trade routes that connected the Arabian Peninsula with the Indian Ocean.

The emergence of communities in the interior and along the shore marks the beginning of Oman's earliest known civilization, which dates back to the third millennium BCE. The Sumerians, Babylonians, and Assyrians affected the area because they were drawn to its priceless resources, including frankincense, myrrh, and copper.

The region saw the birth of the Omani civilization in the first millennium BCE, which built trading networks across the Arabian Sea and the Indian Ocean. Omani sailors travelled great distances, going as far as Southeast Asia, East Africa, and India. The Omanis' nautical prowess brought prosperity to the area, encouraging the growth of significant ports and coastal cities.

Oman has been influenced historically by a number of empires and civilizations. The Portuguese arrived in the 16th century with the aim of controlling the lucrative spice trade. In the late 17th century, the Omani ruler Ahmad bin Said Al-Busaidi overthrew the forts and castles they had built along the coast. Sultan Qaboos bin Said Al Said was a pivotal character in modern Omani history, and the Al-Busaidi dynasty, often known as the Al Said, has controlled Oman ever since.

Oman's culture is strongly influenced by its Islamic past, and the Ibadi sect of Islam is practised by the majority of the country's people. Islam's tenets permeate many aspects of daily life, influencing Omani society's values, customs, and social structure. Mosques are not just places of worship but also hubs for social events and education because of their spectacular architectural architecture.

Omani culture traditionally places a strong emphasis on charity and hospitality towards visitors. Warm smiles, aromatic coffee, and dates are frequently offered as welcome gestures to visitors visiting Oman. The customs of the Omani people, which have been passed down through the centuries, are something they are proud of. The dishdasha for men and the abaya for women are examples of traditional clothing that is still proudly worn, especially during important events and religious celebrations.

The history and culture of Oman have been significantly influenced by the frankincense trade. The Dhofar region in the south of the nation is famed for producing premium frankincense, also referred to as the "scent of Arabia." This fragrant resin has a long history of use in traditional medicine, perfumery, and religious ceremonies. The fact that Oman has a long history with this priceless product is attested to by the historic Frankincense Trail, which runs from Dhofar to the markets of the Mediterranean.

Traditional arts and crafts in Oman also exhibit elements of its cultural heritage. Silverware, ceramics, weaving, and woodwork are a few examples of the crafts that demonstrate the talent and inventiveness of Omani artists. Visitors can browse bustling souks (markets) where they can buy distinctive handmade goods as gifts or souvenirs.

Oman has worked hard in recent years to protect its cultural heritage and encourage tourism while striking a careful balance with contemporary advancements. Forts, castles, and ancient monuments, some of which have undergone painstaking restoration, are accessible to the public and provide a window into Oman's rich past.

Overall, Oman's history and culture are a fascinating fusion of Islamic traditions, maritime prowess, and ancient civilizations. This distinctive tapestry continues to influence the nation's identity and offers tourists a breathtaking window into its recent past.

Climate and Weather

The majority of Oman's climate is dry, with hot summers and mild winters. However, the country's varied geography has led to differences in climate in various parts of the country. Planning your trip and ensuring a comfortable and pleasurable experience depend on your ability to comprehend the Omani environment and weather patterns.

Oman typically has two distinct seasons: a hot summer season and a cool winter season. The summer season normally lasts from April through October, with June through August being the hottest months. Especially in the interior and desert regions, temperatures can skyrocket at this time, with daytime highs exceeding 40°C (104°F). Temperatures in the coastal regions, which include Muscat and Salalah, often range from 30°C to 35°C (86°F to 95°F). Along the seaside, particularly in the summer, humidity levels are relatively high.

In Oman, winter lasts from November to March. Even though summer heat is often more intense, winter temperatures can still be nice for outdoor activities. Average temperatures in coastal locations range from 20°C to 25°C (68°F to 77°F), whereas interior regions and mountains typically experience milder temperatures, with daytime highs of 15°C (59°F) and occasionally even lower lows.

The monsoon season in Oman, also known as the Khareef, is a unique weather occurrence. Between June and September, it takes place in the southern part of Dhofar, most specifically in the vicinity of Salalah. The area experiences heavy rainfall during this period, turning the generally dry landscapes into lush flora. An exceptional chance to appreciate Oman's natural beauty in a new way is provided by the Khareef season.

It is significant to note that Oman's varied geography affects localized climates throughout the nation. Compared to interior regions, coastal places are more comfortable due to the cooling influence of sea breezes. Winters are cooler in the

Al Hajar Mountains, which include Jebel Akhdar and Jebel Shams, and there may even be snowfall on occasion.

It is wise to plan your trip to Oman with the environment and weather in mind, taking into account your chosen activities. The winter is typically the best time of year to travel, go hiking and camping in the mountains, and explore cities and their neighborhoods. The summer is a great time to go on beach vacations and engage in watersports like snorkeling and scuba diving. But it's crucial to take the proper measures, like drinking plenty of water, using sunscreen, and scheduling outside activities for cooler times of the day.

Oman offers a wide variety of landscapes and experiences that may be enjoyed all year long, regardless of the season. Travelers looking for both natural beauty and cultural immersion will find it to be a riveting location thanks to its varying climate and weather conditions, which offer plenty of options for exploration, adventure, and relaxation.

Planning Your Trip

The Best Time to Go

The best time to travel to Oman will largely depend on the activities you enjoy and the areas you want to see. Due to the good weather and milder temperatures, the winter season, which lasts from November to March, is typically regarded as the busiest travel period. This is the perfect season to go sightseeing in cities, see historical places, and enjoy outdoor pursuits like hiking, camping, and wildlife watching.

Plan your trip between June and September if you want to see the Khareef season in Salalah and the Dhofar region. This is the time of year when the area is covered in lush vegetation and cool rain, which produces a distinctive and lovely landscape.

It's crucial to remember that the winter season is also the busiest for tourists, especially in well-known locales like Muscat and the coastline districts. So, if you want to avoid crowds and have a more relaxing time, think about going in the spring (April and May) or the fall (October), which are the shoulder seasons. The weather is still beautiful at these times, and you can benefit from cheaper hotel rates and fewer crowds.

Visa Conditions

Check the visa requirements for your place of citizenship before travelling to Oman. Oman provides a variety of visas, including transit, business, and tourist visas. For a limited time, some nationalities may be eligible for visa-free travel or visas issued at the airport.

The majority of people find getting a tourist visa to be a simple procedure. It may be obtained upon arrival at specific Oman entry ports or in advance through the Royal Oman Police eVisa website. The length of a tourist visa can range from 10 to 30 days, and there are single-entry and multiple-entry options available.

It is advised to visit the Royal Oman Police's official website or contact the Omani embassy or consulate in your area for further details on visa requirements and application processes.

Tips for Health and Safety

Oman generally has low crime rates and a friendly attitude, making it a safe place to travel. To ensure a safe and healthy vacation, it is always crucial to take the appropriate precautions:

1. Keep up with the most recent travel warnings and heed any instructions or suggestions given by your government or other relevant authorities.
2. Keep up with regular hand washing, especially before eating, and maintain good personal hygiene.
3. For drinking and tooth brushing, use bottled water or purified water.
4. By using sunscreen, a hat, and light, breathable clothing, you can stay safe from the sun.

5. Respect local traditions and dress modestly, especially while visiting places of worship.
6. Be aware of your surroundings and take the necessary safety precautions to protect your belongings, especially in crowded places or popular tourist destinations.
7. Having complete travel insurance that pays for medical costs as well as emergency evacuation or repatriation is advised.
8. Additionally, it is advised that you get advice from a medical expert or travel clinic prior to your journey to Oman in order to receive any vaccines or prescriptions that may be required based on your personal health and the length of your stay.

Exchange rates and money

The Omani Rial (OMR) serves as Oman's official currency. 1,000 baisa are used to further split the rial. One rial, five rials, ten rials, twenty rials, and fifty rials are the values of banknotes, while five baisa, ten baisa, twenty baisa, fifty baisa, and one hundred baisa are the values of coins.

It is recommended to exchange your money into Omani rials at the airport or at banks and exchange offices found in major cities when you arrive. Most hotels, restaurants, and bigger institutions accept major credit cards, and ATMs are widely available across the nation. Carrying some cash is advised, especially when visiting smaller businesses or distant locations where card acceptance may be patchy.

Oman's transportation

Oman has an excellent transportation infrastructure that makes it simple to travel around the nation and experience its numerous regions.

1. Car rental: One common way to independently explore Oman is to rent a car. Driving is done on the right side of the road, and there are numerous domestic and international vehicle rental agencies in the nation. Major highways link cities and towns in Oman, which has a modern and well-maintained road network. However, it's crucial to become familiar with local traffic laws and drive carefully, especially when traveling off-road or in isolated locations.

2. Taxis: In metropolitan areas, taxis are easily accessible and can be either flagged down on the street or reserved at authorized taxi stops. Metered taxis and private hiring services like Uber and Careem are available in large cities like Muscat. Prior to beginning the trip, it is advisable to negotiate the fee or use the meter.

3. Public Transportation: In Oman, public buses offer an affordable option for getting around the country's cities. Bus services that connect different locations throughout the nation are run by the Oman National Transport Company. In addition, shared taxis, also known as "Baiza" or "Hiace," are widely used for local travel within cities and villages.

4. Domestic Flights: Oman has a number of domestic airports, making domestic travel a practical way to swiftly visit remote areas. The two principal airlines that fly domestic routes are Oman Air and SalamAir.

5. Ferries: The coastline of Oman offers chances for ferry transport. Between Muscat and the surrounding coastal communities of Khasab and Shinas,

there are frequent ferry services. The Daymaniyat Islands and Masirah Island are also accessible via ferry.

It is recommended to keep travel times and distances between places in mind when organizing your transportation in Oman. Additionally, it's critical to examine the status of the roads and any travel warnings, especially before traveling into off-road or mountainous terrain.

Exploring Muscat

Highlights of Muscat City

The colourful and alluring location of Muscat, the capital of Oman, offers a fusion of old-world charm and modern conveniences. Some of the city's attractions that you shouldn't miss are listed below:

- Al Jalali and Al Mirani Forts: These magnificent forts, which proudly overlook the harbour from the hills above, are evidence of Muscat's historical importance. They don't have a public entrance, yet they make a beautiful backdrop for the city skyline.

- Al Alam Palace is a magnificent example of Islamic architecture and serves as Sultan Qaboos' main palace. The palace, which is located in the center of Old Muscat, is a famous landmark recognized for its eye-catching blue and gold façade. From the outside, visitors may admire the palace and take beautiful pictures.

- Al Riyam Park is a well-liked recreation area with expansive views of the city's coastline, and it is close to Mutrah Corniche. It's the perfect spot for unwinding, having a picnic, or taking a leisurely stroll.

- Qurum Beach is a well-liked destination for both locals and tourists alike. It is situated in the Qurum region. It's the perfect place for a leisurely day by the sea thanks to its golden sands, crystal-clear waters, and gorgeous promenade.

Sultan Qaboos Grand Mosque

One of Muscat's most recognizable structures and a wonderful example of Islamic architecture is the Sultan Qaboos Grand Mosque. Named after the late Sultan Qaboos bin Said al-Said, this magnificent mosque is an architectural wonder that highlights the nation's rich cultural legacy.

The mosque's magnificent facade, which includes ornate Islamic geometric patterns, minarets, and a central dome, mesmerizes visitors. The interior is similarly spectacular, with a huge crystal chandelier and a hand-woven Persian carpet that covers the whole floor in the main prayer hall. The peaceful environment of the mosque encourages reflection.

Outside of prayer times, non-Muslim tourists are free to tour the mosque and admire its magnificent architecture and serene atmosphere. However, it's crucial to dress modestly, with men wearing long shirts and slacks and women covering their hair and donning long sleeves, skirts, or pants.

Corniche and Souq of Mutrah

A look at the traditional Omani way of life can be had by visiting the Mutrah Corniche and Souq. The port and the Mutrah Fort can both be seen beautifully from the waterfront promenade known as the corniche.

The Mutrah Souq, a colourful marketplace next to the corniche where you can immerse yourself in the lively atmosphere and explore a maze of narrow lanes packed with stores selling a range of things, is nearby. The souq is well-known for its traditional Omani handicrafts, which include frankincense, jewellery, textiles, and pottery. It's the ideal location for finding one-of-a-kind gifts and taking in the bustle of an authentic Arabian market.

Muscat's Royal Opera House

It is strongly advised for everyone with an interest in the performing arts to pay the Royal Opera House in Muscat a visit. Opera, ballet, classical music concerts, and theatrical shows are all presented at this top-notch cultural centre, which features a fusion of traditional Omani and modern architectural styles.

The magnificent auditorium offers a great environment for artistic events because of its complex detailing and opulent furniture. Even if you choose not to see a performance, it is worthwhile to visit the opera house to take in its gorgeous architecture and explore the beautifully landscaped gardens that surround it.

Bait Al Zubair Museum

A fascinating tour through Oman's history and culture is provided by the Bait Al Zubair Museum. This private museum, which is situated in the centre of Old Muscat, houses a sizable collection of antiquities, clothes, jewellery, weapons, and historical documents.

You can discover more about Oman's rich cultural history, customs, and historical development. The museum also has exhibitions on Omani architecture, old manuscripts, and exhibits that shed light on the many cultural customs of the various Omani districts.

You can gain a deeper understanding of Oman's past and present by exploring Bait Al Zubair Museum, which enables you to appreciate the nation's distinct identity and cultural tapestry.

Coastal Delights

Sohar

The ancient city of Sohar, which is situated on Oman's northern shore, is rich in historical significance. It is of considerable historical significance because Sindbad the Sailor was born there and because it was once a major trading harbour. Here are some of Sohar's highlights:

The magnificent Sohar Fort is a monument to the city's historical importance. This well-preserved fort, which dates to the 13th century, provides information about the area's past. The spectacular architecture, battlements, and on-site museum can all be explored by guests.

Sohar Souq: Get lost in the lively ambience of Sohar Souq to learn about the customs of the Omani markets. Spices, fabrics, traditional handicrafts, fresh vegetables, and many more products are available in this crowded market.

The gorgeous Sohar Corniche, which spans along the shoreline, is a lovely place to take a leisurely stroll. The Corniche is a great place to unwind and take in the welcoming atmosphere thanks to its stunning sea views, well-kept gardens, and recreational areas.

Sur and the Turtle Reserve

The town of Sur on Oman's east coast is well-known for its lengthy maritime heritage and ancient dhow-building business. The top attractions in Sur are listed below:

Dhow Factory: Sur is well known for its talented artisans, who still construct traditional wooden dhows by hand nowadays.

At the dhow yards, where these imposing vessels are created using age-old techniques, visitors may see the complex process of dhow construction in action.

Sur Maritime Museum: The Sur Maritime Museum offers information about the city's maritime history.

Models of traditional boats, navigational aids, and items from Oman's nautical past are among the exhibits on display in the museum.

Ras Al Jinz Turtle Reserve: The Ras Al Jinz Turtle Reserve is a must-see location for nature lovers and is only a short drive from Sur.

The threatened green turtles live there and come ashore to deposit their eggs. During the nesting season, visitors can sign up for guided excursions to see these fascinating creatures in their native habitat.

Wadi Shab

In Oman's Al Sharqiyah region, there lies a breathtaking natural wonder called Wadi Shab. It is a charming wadi (valley) highlighted by emerald-colored ponds, striking rock formations, and dense flora. What you can do at Wadi Shab is as follows:

Swim and Hike: Take a hike into the wadi, following the clearly designated track as it passes through palm groves, clifftops, and crystal-clear pools.

You'll come across a number of bathing holes as you explore, where you can cool down in the cool water.

Cave exploration is one of Wadi Shab's highlights. Here, you can see the renowned "Hidden Cave."

You must swim through a small gap in the rocks to get to the cave, and after that, you must pass through several chambers with breathtaking natural formations. You'll be rewarded inside the cave with a lovely waterfall and a peaceful environment.

Scenic Beauty: The amazing natural beauty of Wadi Shab will be all around you as you travel. A captivating environment that is perfect for photography and for making enduring memories is created by the contrast between the rocky cliffs, lush vegetation, and blue lakes.

Peninsula of Musandam

The Musandam Peninsula, also referred to as the "Norway of Arabia," is a breathtaking area found on Oman's northernmost tip.

Here are some of this special place's highlights:

Dhow Cruises: Take a traditional dhow sail to see the magnificent fjords of Musandam. Sail along the calm waters while being encircled by high cliffs, striking rock formations, and clean seas.

Swimming, snorkelling, and dolphin viewing are all things you can do while travelling.

Visit the centuries-old fortification that overlooks the city of Khasab, Khasab Castle. The castle houses a museum where visitors may explore the past and present of the Musandam region while also taking in expansive views of the surroundings.

In the centre of the Musandam fjords is an abandoned British telegraph outpost called Telegraph Island. Learn about its intriguing history here. Enjoy snorkelling in the clean seas surrounding the island while exploring the ruins.

Outdoor Recreation: Musandam provides opportunities for hikers, rock climbers, and kayakers to partake in these sports. Adventurers will find it to be a paradise because of the rough terrain and unspoiled natural beauty.

Salalah and the region of Dhofar

The tropical beauty of Salalah, the Dhofar region's capital, lies tucked between the Arabian Sea and the majestic Dhofar Mountains. Salalah, known for its beautiful scenery, distinctive Khareef season, and extensive history, provides a variety of attractions:

Visit the UNESCO World Heritage Site of Al Baleed Archaeological Park to learn more about this ancient port city that dates back to the 12th century.

Visit the preserved ruins, such as the Al Baleed Museum, to learn more about the area's maritime history and the frankincense trade in antiquity.

Khareef Season: You may enjoy Salalah's distinctive Khareef season if you travel there between June and September. The area turns into a lush sanctuary during this time, complete with foggy mountains, tumbling waterfalls, and blossoming flowers. It's the ideal time of year to take advantage of the nice weather, outdoor activities, and splendour of nature.

The Frankincense Land Museum can help you understand more about Oman's involvement in the frankincense trade.

Learn about the long-standing commerce in this fragrant resin in the area, its history, cultivation, and cultural significance.

Enjoy the unspoiled beauty of Mughsayl Beach, which is renowned for its white sands and turquoise waters.

The blowholes, where strong water jets shoot up from beneath caverns to create a stunning display, should not be missed.

Discover the picturesque Jebel Samhan mountain range, which provides sweeping views of the region's lowlands and beaches.

The rough terrain is perfect for off-road excursions and hiking.

Salalah and the Dhofar region, with their beautiful landscapes, rich cultural heritage, and amazing natural occurrences, provide a distinctive and different experience from the rest of Oman.

Majestic Mountains

Jebel Shams

The highest summit in the Al Hajar mountain range, Jebel Shams, popularly known as the "Mountain of the Sun," provides spectacular views and exhilarating outdoor excursions. The highlights of Jebel Shams are listed below:

Grand Canyon of Oman: Wadi Ghul, Oman's equivalent of the Grand Canyon, is located in Jebel Shams.

A beautiful scene that is ideal for trekking and photography is created by the rocky cliffs and narrow canyons. You will be in awe of the size and grandeur of the natural formations as you stand on the edge of the canyon.

The Balcony Walk, a picturesque hiking track that leads you along the canyon's rim, is one of the most popular things to do in Jebel Shams.

Adventure seekers will never forget the stunning views of the nearby mountains and valleys that the trail offers.

The settlement of Al Hamra is renowned for its restored traditional mud-brick homes and is situated at the foot of Jebel Shams.

Explore the Bait Al Safah Museum, meander around the winding lanes, and get a sense of the tradition and culture of the area.

Jebel Akhdar

The mountain range known as Jebel Akhdar, or "Green Mountain," is renowned for its cooler weather, terraced fields, and breathtaking natural beauty. What to anticipate in Jebel Akhdar is as follows:

Jebel Akhdar's Saiq Plateau is a scenic area known for its rose gardens, fruit orchards, and terraced farms.

A serene and peaceful mood is created by the plateau's breathtaking panoramic views of the nearby mountains and deep wadis.

Rose Harvesting: Jebel Akhdar is well-known for its rose gardens, rose water, and other items made from roses. You may observe the traditional method of rose picking and distillation during the flowering season, which is typically from March to May. It is an enthralling sight and fills the air with a pleasant floral scent.

Nature Trails and Hiking: Jebel Akhdar is a haven for hikers and outdoor enthusiasts. In addition to providing beautiful views and the chance to explore the area's rich flora and fauna, the mountains are home to a number of paths. Every type of hiker will find a trail that suits them, from easy strolls to strenuous treks.

Traditional Villages: Al Ayn and Wadi Bani Habib are two traditional mountain villages in Jebel Akhdar where you may get a feel for the traditional Omani way of life. Discover the local cultures and traditions by exploring the tiny alleyways, visiting the historic falaj irrigation systems, and mingling with the kind inhabitants.

Al Hajar Mountains

Northern Oman is home to the Al Hajar Mountains, which form a striking backdrop to the nation's landscapes. The primary features of this mountain range are as follows:

Climbing: For those who enjoy trekking and climbing, the Al Hajar Mountains provide amazing chances. There are alternatives for climbers of all experience levels, from easy trails appropriate for novices to difficult ones. Adventurers flock to it because of the craggy terrain, steep peaks, and deep wadis.

With a height of more than 1,800 metres, Jebel Misht is one of the Al Hajar Mountains' most recognisable peaks. Climbers who want a difficult ascent and breathtaking views from the summit frequently travel there.

Geological Wonders: The Al Hajar Mountains are noteworthy in terms of their geology, displaying interesting rock formations and prehistoric fossils. The area offers prospects for geological study and discovery due to its limestone cliffs, deep gorges, and unique geological characteristics.

Jebel Akhdar and Jebel Shams: The Al Hajar Mountains are home to the previously mentioned Jebel Akhdar and Jebel Shams. When exploring the area, it is important to visit these peaks since they provide distinctive experiences.

Nizwa and Bahla

The historical cities of Nizwa and Bahla are situated in Oman's interior. They are renowned for both their magnificent architecture and rich cultural legacy. What you can discover in Nizwa and Bahla is listed below:

Nizwa Fort: Nizwa is home to Nizwa Fort, one of Oman's most well-known forts. This majestic building, which dates back to the 17th century, serves as a reminder of the city's historical importance. In addition to learning about the history and military tactics of the area, visitors can explore the fort's unique architecture and climb the tower for panoramic views.

Nizwa Souq: The bustling Nizwa Souq, a traditional market that provides an insight into daily life in Oman, is located next to Nizwa Fort. Explore the stalls selling traditional Omani items, silver jewellery, handicrafts, and spices that line the small alleyways. The Friday cattle market, when locals congregate to buy and sell livestock, is one of the souq's most well-known attractions.

Bahla Fort is a renowned mud-brick stronghold that dates back to the 13th century and is included as part of the UNESCO World Heritage Site. The fort's imposing walls and elaborate layout highlight traditional Omani design. Although the fort is now undergoing restoration, visitors can still enjoy the exterior and discover its historical value.

Discover the lovely Bahla Oasis, a quiet oasis in the middle of the desert. The oasis is renowned for its historic falaj irrigation systems, date palm trees, and traditional mud-brick homes. Walk gently through the palm groves to experience the tranquil atmosphere of this lush oasis.

A look at Oman's rich history, beautiful architecture, and way of life can be found in Nizwa and Bahla. The cultural heritage of the nation would be better understood after visiting these cities.

Desert Adventures

Wahiba Sands

In the eastern part of Oman, there is a large desert called Wahiba Sands, also called Sharqiya Sands.

It is renowned for its vast expanses of golden sand dunes, distinctive desert wildlife, and the chance to encounter traditional Bedouin culture. What to anticipate at Wahiba Sands is as follows:

Sandboarding and Dune Bashing: In a 4x4 vehicle, explore the imposing sand dunes of Wahiba Sands and take part in the exhilarating adventure sport of dune bashing. For an adrenaline rush, you may also attempt sandboarding, which involves riding a board down the dunes' slopes.

Bedouin Camps: Spend the night in a genuine Bedouin camp in the middle of the desert to fully experience the Bedouin lifestyle.

Comfortable lodging in traditional tents is available in Bedouin camps, where you may savour Arabian hospitality, delectable regional cuisine, and cultural performances under the starry desert sky.

Wildlife that has adapted to the desert calls Wahiba Sands home. Watch out for desert foxes, sand gazelles, Arabian oryx, and a variety of birds. The particular flora and fauna of the desert habitat can also be learned about.

The Empty Quarter, or Rub' al Khali

The Empty Quarter, commonly known as Rub' al Khali, is the world's biggest continuous sand desert, extending into Yemen, Oman, Saudi Arabia, and the United Arab Emirates. It is a vast, inaccessible desert that exudes a supernatural splendor. What you can find in the empty quarter is as follows:

Remote Desert Expeditions: Travel deep into Rub' al Khali on an extraordinary desert excursion. These adventures frequently entail driving across the sand dunes in specially designed vehicles while being escorted by knowledgeable guides. You'll get a chance to experience the desert's vastness and discover its secret passageways.

Starry Nights: The Empty Quarter boasts some of the purest, darkest, and unpolluted night skies. Camping in the desert at night will leave you spellbound by the sky's profusion of stars, which together form an amazing celestial show.

Bedouin Customs and Culture

Exploring Oman offers the chance to discover more about the distinctive culture and traditions of the Bedouin people, who have a long history in the region. You can encounter the following features of Bedouin culture:

Bedouin hospitality is renowned for being friendly and welcoming. When you visit Bedouin settlements or camps, you may take advantage of their genuine hospitality, which frequently entails tasting local cuisine, sipping Arabic coffee, and conversing with them about their way of life.

Traditional Clothing: Bedouin women typically wear vibrant costumes and headscarves, while men typically wear the dishdasha, a long white robe, and the kumma, a cap. You might get the chance to dress as a Bedouin and participate in cultural events.

Known for their complex weaving, needlework, and handicrafts, Bedouins are accomplished artisans. Traditional craft demonstrations, such as making elaborate textile patterns or weaving carpets, are available for you to see and take part in.

Camel trekking and desert camping

Exploring the deserts of Oman must include camping in the desert and going on camel treks. Here's what to anticipate:

Spend a night camping in the desert beneath a starry sky while being surrounded by the serenity of the sand dunes. Whether in the Wahiba Sands or the Rub' al Khali, desert camps provide cozy lodgings, home-cooked meals, cultural shows, and the chance to relax in the serene desert atmosphere.

Camel Trekking: Go on a camel journey and travel across the desert landscapes like the ancient Bedouins did. As you go through the desert, take in the rhythmic sway of the camel's pace and the breathtaking grandeur of the sand dunes from a different perspective.

You may experience the traditional Bedouin way of life, connect with the immensity of nature, and make priceless memories in the Arabian deserts through desert excursions in Oman.

Cultural Experiences

Castles and Forts

Oman is home to a large number of forts and castles that highlight the nation's extensive history and magnificent architecture. Visit some of these well-known ones:

Nizwa Fort: This well-known fort, which is part of the city of Nizwa, is a UNESCO World Heritage Site and provides insight into Oman's military past. Examine the elaborate design and imposing walls, and climb to the top for sweeping views of the city.

Jabrin Castle is a must-see because of its exquisite interior decorations and elaborate ceilings.

It contains chambers that have been preserved effectively, such as a courtroom, residential quarters, and a library.

Bahla Fort: This mud-brick fort is another UNESCO World Heritage Site and is located in Bahla. Admire its majestic design and discover its importance in Omani history.

Rustaq Fort: This fort, which is a part of the town of Rustaq, is renowned for both its stunning architecture and historical significance. Discover the fort's courtyards, towers, and displays that highlight the fort's contribution to the area's defence.

Customary Omani Food

The flavours of Arabian, Persian, Indian, and East African culinary traditions are delightfully merged into Omani cuisine. To sample, try the following foods and gourmet experiences:

Shuwa: In this typical Omani meal, marinated meat—usually lamb or goat—is slow-cooked for hours in a sand oven. The outcome is juicy, delicate meat that is frequently consumed on special occasions.

Majboos is a flavorful rice dish that is frequently served with marinated meat or fish and is prepared with a mixture of spices, including saffron, cardamom, and turmeric.

Mashuai is a well-known Omani cuisine that consists of a well-cooked entire lamb or fish that has been grilled in a spice marinade. The meat is delicate and tasty, and aromatic rice is frequently paired with it.

The traditional sweet dish from Oman is prepared with sugar, rosewater, ghee, saffron, and nuts. Arabic coffee is frequently served with Omani halwa, which is well known for its creamy and sticky texture.

Dates: Oman is well known for its premium dates, which are an essential component of Omani cuisine. You can sample various kinds of dates and even go to a date plantation to see how dates are picked.

Frankincense Trail

Frankincense has been produced and traded for a very long time in Oman. The Frankincense Trail takes you on a tour of the historic locations and trade routes connected to this priceless resin. Here are some things you can discover on the trail:

Visit the UNESCO World Heritage Site of Wadi Dawkah, which is well-known for its huge groves of frankincense trees. Learn about frankincense planting and harvesting while exploring the historic ruins.

Al Balid Archaeological Park: Al Balid Archaeological Park, which is in Salalah, was formerly a significant harbour and frankincense trading centre. To learn about the significance of this trade historically and culturally, explore the ruins and go to the Frankincense Land Museum.

Shisr/Wubar Archaeological Site: This prehistoric location is thought to be the location of Ubar, a lost metropolis also referred to as the "Atlantis of the Sands." It is referenced in historical records and traditions as a significant hub for the frankincense trade.

Omani trinkets and crafts

Don't pass up the chance to purchase one-of-a-kind Omani crafts and souvenirs when visiting the country. Here are some things to think about:

The Omani Khanjar is a traditional dagger and a representation of national pride. Khanjars made of silver that are expertly constructed and have elaborately carved handles and sheaths are readily available.

Omani ladies are renowned for their love of silver jewellery. Look for gorgeous jewellery with traditional Omani patterns, such as necklaces, earrings, bracelets, and rings.

Frankincense and Incense Burners: Use frankincense resin or incense sticks to bring the wonderful essence of Oman home. Additionally, incense burners with elaborate designs can be found made of clay or brass.

Omani textiles: Beautiful souvenirs can be made from Omani textiles, such as their vibrant shawls and embroidered clothing. Look for rugs, scarves, and traditional Omani attire that have been handcrafted.

Customary Festivals in Oman

Oman celebrates a number of traditional festivals all year long, giving tourists an opportunity to experience the colourful culture and traditions of the nation. A few notable festivals are listed below:

Annually, the capital city of Muscat hosts the **Muscat Festival**, whichhonourss Omani culture with exhibits, traditional performances, handicrafts, and food vendors. It provides a thorough understanding of Omani culture.

Salalah Tourism Celebration: This celebration, which takes place in Salalah, honours the Khareef monsoon season. It includes cultural shows, traditional music and dance, and exhibits showcasing the distinctive customs and unmatched beauty of the area.

Nizwa Date Event: This event honours the significance of dates in Omani culture and is held in Nizwa. It displays several date types, customary date-picking contests, and cultural acts.

Festivals celebrating camel racing are held in Oman, particularly in the winter. Traditional camel races take place during these festivals, displaying the nation's love of these majestic animals.

You may experience traditional Omani music, dance, cuisine, and customs by attending these festivals, providing a unique cultural experience while you are there.

Outdoor Activities

Snorkelling and Scuba Diving

Divers and snorkelers will find beautiful underwater scenery and a variety of marine life along Oman's coastline. Here are some of Oman's best diving and snorkelling locations:

Daymaniyat Islands: The Daymaniyat Islands are a marine reserve that is protected off the coast of Muscat.

It is well renowned for its pristine seas, brilliant coral reefs, and variety of marine

life, including turtles, rays, and colourful reef fish.

Musandam Peninsula: The United Arab Emirates separates the Musandam Peninsula from the remainder of Oman, which is known for its stunning fjords and a variety of marine life. Discover an underwater world teeming with marine life, including tropical fish, dolphins, and occasionally a whale shark, by diving or snorkelling in the seas surrounding the peninsula.

Hallaniyat Islands: The Hallaniyat Islands, which are off the coast of southern Oman, provide excellent diving and snorkelling opportunities. Discover unspoiled coral reefs, come across schools of fish, and spot a variety of marine life, such as turtles and moray eels.

Dolphin Observation

Numerous dolphin species may be found in Oman's waterways, and dolphin-watching excursions provide visitors with the chance to see these lively and intelligent animals in their natural environment. Here are some of the best places to see dolphins in Oman:

Take a dolphin-watching cruise out of Muscat and into the Arabian Sea to see pods of dolphins playing in the waves and leaping.

Musandam Peninsula: The dolphin populations in the waters near the Musandam Peninsula are renowned for being thriving. Embark on a boat cruise from Khasab and take in the breathtaking fjords while you observe dolphins up close.

Dhofar Coast: You can go on dolphin-watching expeditions to see spinner dolphins and other species in their natural habitat around the southern coast of Oman, particularly close to Salalah.

Trekking and hiking

The varied landscapes of Oman provide good opportunities for trekkers and hikers. Here are a few of Oman's well-liked places for hiking and trekking:

Jebel Shams: Often referred to as the "Grand Canyon of Oman," Jebel Shams features breathtaking hiking paths that meander through untamed valleys and spectacular cliff faces. The area offers breathtaking views and exhilarating trekking opportunities because it is home to Oman's tallest peak.

Jebel Akhdar: Also referred to as the "Green Mountain," Jebel Akhdar is renowned for its terraced farmland, ancient towns, and breathtaking vistas. Explore the charming villages, hike along the mountain trails, and take in the green surroundings and mild climate.

Wadi Shab is a lovely valley with waterfalls and blue swimming pools. Discover hidden caves and beautiful scenery as you hike around the wadi's rugged terrain, swim through natural pools, and more.

Al Jabal Al Akhdar: Situated in the Al Hajar mountain range, Al Jabal Al Akhdar has a number of hiking paths that take visitors to picturesque vistas, terraced crops, and traditional communities. Discover the area's natural splendour and become immersed in Omani mountain culture.

Rock Climbing

Rock climbers can find plenty of possibilities in Oman's hilly terrain. Here are some popular spots for rock climbing in Oman:

Jebel Misht: Jebel Misht, which is in the Jebel Akhdar region, offers difficult rock climbing routes for both novice and expert climbers.

A thrilling climbing experience is offered by the limestone cliffs amid stunning natural scenery.

Jebel Qamar is a mountain range in the Musandam Peninsula notable for its imposing cliffs and untamed rock formations. There are numerous routes available for climbers of all skill levels, and they may take in expansive views of the nearby fjords while doing so.

With its stunning cliffs and difficult climbs, Wadi Bani Auf, which is part of the Al Hajar mountain range, is a well-liked spot for rock climbing. While appreciating the breathtaking wadi scenery, climbers can test their abilities on the vertical cliffs.

Watersports

Oman is a haven for lovers of watersports because of its immaculate shoreline and crystal-clear waters. Here are some well-liked water sports you may participate in in Oman:

Kitesurfing and windsurfing: Oman's coastal regions, including Muscat and Salalah, provide ideal conditions for these sports. As you float above the ocean and ride the waves, feel the wind's force.

Standing up and kayaking Paddleboarding: Use a kayak or a stand-up paddleboard to explore the calm coastal waters of Oman. Get up close to marine life as you paddle around rocky cliffs and glide through isolated bays.

Jet skiing and parasailing are two thrilling activities that will give you an adrenaline rush. While jet skiing across open water or parasailing high above the coast, you can take in panoramic views of the ocean and coastline.

Fishing aficionados will love Oman because of its waters' abundance of marine life. Embark on a fishing excursion and try your hand at snagging some of the local fish species, such as barracuda, kingfish, or tuna.

'Whatever your interests in adventure are—underwater exploration, dolphin encounters, strenuous hiking, thrilling rock climbing, or thrilling watersports—Oman has a wide choice of activities to satisfy them all.

Practical Information

Lodging

You can choose from a range of lodging options in Oman to match your preferences and financial constraints. Here are a few well-liked options:

Luxury Hotels and Resorts: Oman is home to a number of opulent hotels and resorts that provide top-notch amenities, first-rate service, and breathtaking vistas. These places frequently have spa services, a variety of dining alternatives, and entertainment options.

Boutique Hotels: Think about staying at a boutique hotel for a more personalised and distinctive experience. These more intimate businesses provide attentive service, chic furnishings, and a homey atmosphere.

Beach Resorts: The coastline of Oman is lined with lovely beach resorts that give guests easy access to pristine beaches and a variety of water sports. Relax by the pool, take in some riverfront eating, and take in the peace and quiet of the beach.

Desert Camps: Staying at a desert camp will allow you to experience the allure of Oman's deserts. These traditional-style camps offer cozy lodging that lets you fully appreciate the desert environment while taking advantage of starry nights and cultural encounters.

Guesthouses and homestays: Choose a guesthouse or a homestay for a more comprehensive cultural experience. These lodgings provide an opportunity to meet locals, discover Omani culture, and take advantage of local hospitality.

Internet and communication

In Oman, communication and internet connectivity are often reliable. What you need to know is as follows:

Mobile networks: There are a number of mobile network operators in Oman that offer SIM cards and prepaid plans to tourists. In airports, malls, or mobile network outlets, buying a local SIM card is simple.

Internet access: In urban areas, the majority of hotels, resorts, and cafes offer free Wi-Fi to visitors. Major cities and towns also offer internet cafés where you can pay to use the internet.

If you prefer to utilize the cell network in your home country, check with your provider about international roaming packages and tariffs to assure connectivity throughout your visit.

Regional Protocol and Customs

It's crucial to observe local etiquette and customs when visiting Oman. Here are some crucial points:

Dress decently: Oman is a conservative nation, so modest attire is preferred, particularly in public settings. Women should cover their shoulders and knees, and men should wear modest attire.

Salutations: When greeting locals, say "As-salamu alaykum" (peace be upon you) politely and say "Wa alaykum as-salam" (and upon you be peace) in return.

Because Oman is primarily a Muslim country, it is necessary to **observe Islamic traditions**. During the month of Ramadan, refrain from eating, drinking, or smoking in public and pay attention to local prayer schedules.

Public Displays of Affection: It is advised to avoid making public displays of affection in Oman because they are uncommon there.

When **photographing people or groups** of people, especially in more conservative settings or at religious places, you should always get their consent.

Key Arabic Expressions

Although English is widely spoken in Oman, learning a few simple Arabic words can improve your trip and demonstrate respect for the local way of life. The following are some key words:

Good day: Marhaba

I'm grateful. Shukran

True: Na'am

No: La

Please, I'm Fadlik.

I'm sorry. (only used in English) Excuse me

Where are you? Ayna...?

What does this cost: Kam hadha?

I fail to comprehend: The afham

Goodbye: Assalamu alikum

Useful Contact

It's beneficial to have some crucial contact information on hand when you're in Oman. Below are a few helpful contacts:

1. In cases of police, fire, or medical emergencies, dial 999.
2. Call 9999 to reach the Royal Oman Police (ROP)
3. Helpline for the Ministry of Tourism: +968 2412 9286

For contact information and questions particular to your airport, check with them.

Consulate or Embassy: For advice or information, get in touch with the embassy or consulate of your nation in Oman.

It's a good idea to save these phone numbers or write them down for quick access in case of emergencies or questions while you're visiting Oman.

Appendix

Oman Travel Tips

1. Respect the local customs and traditions and dress modestly, especially while visiting religious places or more conservative communities.
2. Stay hydrated and protect yourself from the sun by wearing sunscreen, a hat, and sunglasses.
3. It's advisable to drink bottled water and avoid eating tap water or ice from unknown sources.
4. Carry a copy of your passport, visa, and other necessary travel documents with you at all times.
5. Observe traffic rules and drive carefully if you plan to rent a car in Oman.
6. Bargaining is prevalent in souqs (markets), so feel free to bargain pricing, but do so gently.
7. It's advisable to obtain travel insurance that covers medical bills and emergencies during your vacation.
8. Be cautious when swimming in the sea and observe any posted warnings or advice from lifeguards.
9. Research and reserve activities and lodgings in advance, especially during peak tourist seasons.

Packing List

1. Lightweight, loose-fitting attire that covers your shoulders and knees to respect local norms.

2. Comfortable walking shoes or sandals, especially for exploring historical sites or hiking paths.
3. Swimwear and beach basics are necessary if you wish to enjoy Oman's beaches or resorts.
4. A hat, sunglasses, and sunscreen to protect yourself from the sun's rays.
5. A reusable water container to stay hydrated throughout your travels.
6. Insect repellent, especially if you plan to visit coastal or rural locations.
7. A travel adaptor for charging your electrical devices.
8. A light jacket or shawl for chilly evenings, especially in mountainous settings.
9. Necessary prescriptions, along with a basic first aid kit.
10. Cash and/or credit cards for transactions, as well as some local money (Omani Rial).

Recommended Reading

- "Oman: Politics and Society in the Qaboos State" by Marc Valeri
- "Oman: Under Arabian Skies" by Rory Patrick Allen
- "Oman, UAE, and the Arabian Peninsula" (Lonely Planet Travel Guide)
- "The Immortal City" by Amy Kuivalainen
- "Arabian Sands" by Wilfred Thesiger
- "The Sultan's Shadow: One Family's Rule at the Crossroads of East and West" by Christiane Bird

Maps of Oman

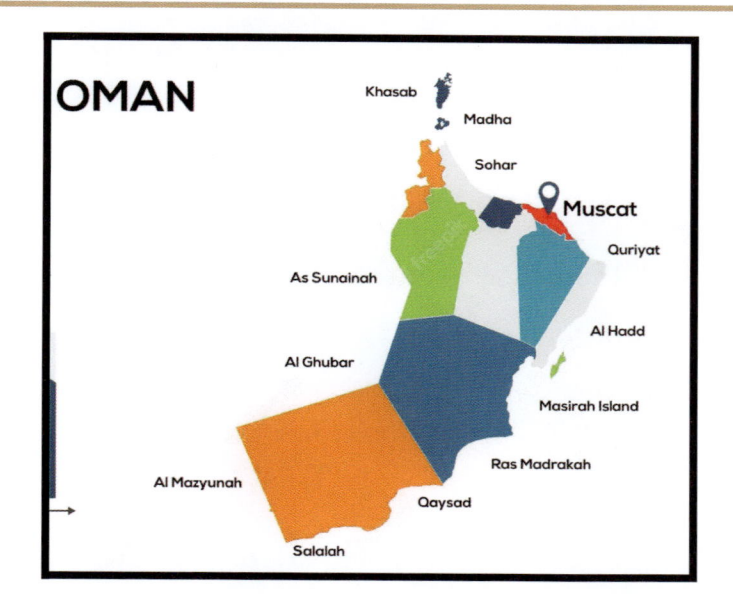

1. Official Oman Tourism website: They provide maps of Oman's various regions, cities, and attractions. (www.omantourism.gov.om)
2. Mobile applications: Download smartphone apps such as Google Maps or Maps.me, which provide detailed maps of Oman that can be used offline.

Conversion Charts

1. Currency Conversion: Carry a currency conversion chart or use a trusted currency converter app to convert Omani Rial (OMR) to your native currency.
2. Measurement Conversion: Consider a measurement conversion chart or app to convert between the metric system used in Oman and other measurement systems used in your home country (e.g., temperature, distance, and weight).

These materials will aid you in organizing your trip, navigating Oman, and ensuring a seamless travel experience.

Printed in Great Britain
by Amazon